FARMALL TRACTORS
in the 1950s

Guy Fay

MBI Publishing Company

First published in 2000 by MBI Publishing Company,
729 Prospect Avenue, PO Box 1, Osceola, WI 54020-0001 USA

MBI Publishing Company books are also available at discounts in
bulk quantity for industrial or sales-promotional use. For details
write to Special Sales Manager at Motorbooks International
Wholesalers & Distributors, 729 Prospect Avenue, Osceola, WI
54020-0001 USA.

Library of Congress Cataloging-in-Publication Data
Fay, Guy.
    Farmall tractors in the 1950s/Guy Fay.
        p. cm. — (Enthusiast color series)
    Includes index.
    ISBN 0-7603-0762-8 (pbk. : alk. paper)
        1. IHC tractors—History. 2. IHC tractors—Pictorial
    works. I. Title. II. Series.
    TL233.6.I38 F3768 2000
    629.225'2—dc21   99-052219

On the front cover: Farmalls in action! This scene, though
seemingly rare and special today, was commonplace in the
1950s. Tractor enthusiasts and researchers are fortunate that
the archives of International Harvester are preserved at the State
Historical Society of Wisconsin. In addition to thousands of
linear feet of sales literature, brochures, and manuscript
material, the archive also contains many photographic gems
like this view of a Stage II Super M with live hydraulics. *State
Historical Society of Wisconsin*

On the frontispiece: It's not an antique tractor show, but rather,
an IH exhibit at the 1955 National Plowing Contest at
Wabash, Indiana. Setting up displays at events like these
around the nation was a great way to expose farmers to the
IH line of tractors and implements. *State Historical Society
of Wisconsin*

On the title page: International Harvester started producing
forage choppers in the 1920s. By the 1940s, they were evolving
into more advanced, practical machines. Of course, when it
came to marketing their products, IH could sell both tractors
and trucks with the same photos. In this case, it's a post-1949
Farmall M and an L-Line truck. *State Historical Society
of Wisconsin*

On the back cover: Somewhere in the dairyland back in the
1950s, this WD-6 was plowing up the earth. Fitted with the
same diesel engine as the MD, WD-6s were initially a popular
choice of farmers. A complicated cylinder head that had
cracking problems caused the WD-6 to soon fall out of favor,
though. *State Historical Society of Wisconsin*

Printed in China

Contents

Acknowledgments

Acknowledgments and sincere thanks go to: Lee Grady, Nicolette Bromberg, David Benjamin, Lisa Hinzman, and Andy Kraushaar of the State Historical Society of Wisconsin; Rich Saraga, Steve Hile, George Vickers, Ettienne Gentil, and Dave Rogers of Case Corporation; and Greg Lennes and Julia Brunni (especially for introducing me to the Cheesecake Factory!) of Navistar International. At MBI Publishing Company, thanks to John Adams-Graf, Lee Klancher, and Jane Mausser. Other assorted miscreants include: Randy Leffingwell, Grandma, Half Price Books, Borders, the crew at Enterprise rent-a-car, and assorted other people who put up with me. It takes a whole lotta people to make a book with one name on it!

Introduction

The McCormick/International Harvester Collection at the State Historical Society of Wisconsin houses an amazing group of material. The collection ranges from the original papers of Cyrus McCormick to photographs of Super 70 tractors produced just before International Harvester (IH) sold the Ag Equipment Division to the Case Corporation. It houses thousands of manuals, more than 100,000 photographs, tons of advertising literature, and large amounts of other corporate literature. Even with this large collection (well over 3,000 cubic yards of materials), there is a surprising amount of information that is lacking in the collection. This, alone, is a testament to the incredible size and the wide-ranging activities of the company.

The research for this work involved material in the collection as well as from the Case Corporation and the Navistar International Transportation Company archives. The photographs in this book all came from the McCormick/International Harvest Collection. IH started using large format color photography after World War II, initially using Kodachrome. This is fortunate for us today, because Kodachrome has excellent preservation qualities. Because the photography was expensive, there was a very limited amount documenting the small production variants like orchard and high crop tractors. This was a pattern which continued to the end of the company's production. In 1951, Kodak discontinued large format Kodachrome, forcing IH to use Ektachrome film. Unlike its predecessor, Ektachrome has proven to have very poor preservation qualities. You may see a reddish tint to some of the photographs, which is the result of aging. Problems like this, and many others, continue to challenge the McCormick/IH Collection at the State Historical Society of Wisconsin as it seeks to preserve the large amounts of materials in its possession. Nevertheless, these materials provide collectors, researchers, and enthusiasts with a rare opportunity to see the tractors and equipment in stunning, original color.

1

1950–1954

Glory Days

The Little Tractors: Cub, Super A , C, Super C, and Super A-1

International Harvester entered the 1950s with hopes of saving the small, family farm with small tractors. The company already had an established line of small tractors produced at the Louisville, Kentucky, Works. The Cub entered production May 15, 1947, and the Super A and C began production in 1948. The philosophy behind small tractor production was that these well-equipped tractors could help part-time farmers in the North run the family farm at night while working a day job. Small farms in the South, still dominated by horses and mules, could improve efficiency by mechanizing their small power needs.

By 1950, however, the initial sales rush for the Cub was gone and the Super A was fading, leaving only the C doing well. To promote sales of the

Most people think of Cubs as small cultivating tractors, but the tractors can do any chore on a small farm. Although belt use was dying out rapidly at that point, Cubs could and were outfitted for belt use, including this nifty little hammer mill. State Historical Society of Wisconsin

9

Louisville tractors, IH capitalized on the year 1950 with the Mid Century Sales promotion. This campaign involved changing the Louisville paint line to shoot white instead of red. The white tractors, after being shipped to the dealerships, were fitted with promotional cardboard inserts for the wheel wells, a sign that perched on the hood, and "Mystick" stars that stuck on various parts of the tractors to describe sales features. Tractors were used extensively at dealership events, and they were hauled out to farms to demonstrate in the field. In September 1950, 72 dealers who won regional sales contests were given a four-day "Winner's Tour" of Louisville Works, seats at a musical, and a trip to the Bears-Eagles NFL game in

Chicago. One dealer reportedly traded tractors for horses and lovebirds to win his region.

Despite the energetic marketing campaign, IH looked at eliminating low-sales tractors in the early 1950s. Industrial tractors were examined. The International Super A industrial had a "heavy-duty" front axle of malleable iron, which was square in section. Testing in early 1952 indicated that the normal Farmall Super A axle made of steel tubing, was equal in strength, so the square front axle was dropped. A summer's mowing by a local customer, the Illinois State Highway Commission, however, revealed problems with the Farmall axle when used with the AI-23 Highway Mower. The old industrial axles made a

The combination of the trademark and model symbol decals identifies this Super A as having been built between July 1949 and 1951. The farm is across the road from IH's Hinsdale, Illinois, test farm. The hay rake looks a lot bigger than the tractor. State Historical Society of Wisconsin

Photos of Super AVs are rare in the archive collection. IH preferred to spend money on expensive color photos of mainstream tractors rather than small production specialty tractors. This pre-1949 Super AV is side dressing fertilizer on a truck farm. State Historical Society of Wisconsin

At one time, International Harvester tried to produce everything a farm needed in the way of equipment, although sometimes reality and slow sales kept the company out of a market. Here's a post-1949 C with a small grinder and an IH barge wagon grinding shell corn. It's staged; that cloud of dust normally isn't there. State Historical Society of Wisconsin

The Farmalls were at home on the corn fields of the Midwest and the cotton fields of the South. This post-1949 H is pulling a four-row corn planter in northern Illinois. State Historical Society of Wisconsin

comeback, but the industrial's days were numbered. Some customer surveys in the early 1950s indicated that dealers wouldn't have minded seeing the Super A disappear forever in favor of the Super C—a strange result for a tractor that would remain in production essentially unchanged until 1980.

Farmers in the early 1950s wanted more horsepower, and the company listened. Among the little tractors, the C was first. A preproduction lot of 500 3 1/8x4-inch bore and stroke engines was prepared for Farmall Cs in a program authorized December 29, 1947. All of these engines were fitted with the new battery ignition (distributor system) that was scheduled to enter production shortly on regular Cs. Serial numbers FC 48000 to 48492 were included, along with FC 50465. The engines were labeled C-122. Carburized bull gears were experimented with to handle the increased power.

The preproduction tractors apparently performed well: The Super C with the C-123 engine entered production in mid-1951. The new Super C also saw the official introduction of disc brakes, although some orchard tractors had been using them for several years, and certain customers may have

The Stage II Super Hs had live hydraulics with the reservoir located under the fuel tank. Super C seat/battery box assemblies were used to relocate the battery. In the 1950s, corn pickers were still by far the most popular way to harvest corn. Soon, combines with corn heads would be invading America. State Historical Society of Wisconsin

Back in the late 1800s, a manure spreader was considered high tech. IH built them as part of the "new lines" starting in about 1905, and built them until the end of the company. This spreader falls right in the middle, with the W-4 being produced after 1949, according to the decal. State Historical Society of Wisconsin

been able to order them as "unlisted options." The new brakes required a variety of other changes, including a new rear frame, brake housings and rods, new bull pinions, and new pedals. The new engine required a new radiator grille and fuel tank assemblies to accommodate the higher capacity radiator needed to cool the larger engine. A new water pump and revised steering were also added.

The Farmall Super A, which had been built with the old C-113 engine long after the Super C received the C-123, finally got the larger engine in 1954. Originally, the plan was to still call the tractors the Super A until production of the Farmall 100 replacement began in late 1954, but management decided to give the tractors a new name, at least for internal use and for production record keeping. The name

Here's a Super W-4 belted to a grinder that's doing its job: grinding cob corn. The rear wheel disc is unusual. The hoses used for the live hydraulics are visible below the belt. The Super W-4 would soon be replaced by the 300 Utility family. State Historical Society of Wisconsin

became the Super A-1, but the only place on the tractor that reflected the nameplate was on the serial number plate. The decals still said "Super A." Super C radiators, hoods, fan housings, fuel tanks and systems, air cleaners, and other miscellaneous parts were installed on the A-1s. New radiator grilles (which used some Super C parts) were made, while the Farmall and International Super A-1 borrowed rear-axle housings from the Super AV. (These housings had

been available for these tractors as service parts.) The rear-axle bearings and differentials were beefed up as well. Steering housings were changed, while the shaft was changed to accommodate the new 18-inch steering wheel.

The Farmall Super C got an interesting new attachment in 1954. The Hydra-Creeper was a slow-speed (1/4-mile per hour) drive that attached to the PTO shaft of the tractor. Inside the unit was a

Using the Old Stuff

Once upon a time, tractors lasted a very short time in the field. Sometimes, they lasted less than a week. The conditions a farm tractor had to face were brutal, and after the early failures, the tractor companies began to build tractors that could take the conditions. By the 1950s, the companies thought that their tractors could last for seven years. As we know now, that number is probably closer to forever. Replaceable sleeves, excellent sealing and pressure lubrication, and filtration of oil and air means that tractors are pretty much unlimited in lifetime, as long as maintenance is performed and periodic overhauls replace components that see heavy wear.

I grew up using Super Ms, C and Super Cs, and Super As in normal farming activities where those tractors were efficient and appropriate. Years later, those tractors are still used in those activities by the neighbor we borrowed from. Old tractors are still efficient as far as purchase cost and size, critical in today's farming economy. In addition, today's "rural" home boom with acre lots or more have created a demand for older tractors for mowing.

There are drawbacks to using older tractors. Fuel efficiency isn't great compared to today's diesel engines. Safety is a major drawback: There's been a lot of progress made in balance, rollover protection (nonexistent on original old tractors, although it can be retrofitted), fuel systems, shields, and other areas. Hitches and hydraulics are major potential problems. Today's standard three-point hitch wasn't found on Farmalls until the late 1950s and can't be retrofitted on certain tractors like the Standards (W-4, W-6, W-9 family). In short, don't think that using an old tractor is as simple as starting it up, or that you can't get killed doing it.

The issues relating to using the older tractors can be daunting if you don't have a farming background. *Antique Tractor Bible*, by Spencer Yost, can help you start out in the right direction. The book is available from MBI Publishing Company.

This is a Super C with a C-254 two-row cultivator and a no. 91 spring-tooth attachment. This photograph, taken in 1953 by William F. Eichmann, is pretty special. It was taken on the Olaf Sage farm near Edgerton, Wisconsin—just a road south of the farm where the author was raised. The house in the background was the home of some folks who worked for the author's family in tobacco at one time. The author's family had a Super C that had identical equipment on it. State Historical Society of Wisconsin

IH started producing forage choppers in the 1920s. By the 1940s, they were getting into more advanced, practical machines. Of course, IH could sell both tractors and trucks with the same photos. It's a post-1949 Farmall M and an L-Line truck with a 1950 Illinois plate. **State Historical Society of Wisconsin**

The MD diesel began production in 1941. It started well in cold weather, but it suffered from reliability problems. IH diesel tractors did not sell well until the 460/560 was introduced in 1958. Note the original dealer decal on the side of the grille. State Historical Society of Wisconsin

hydraulic motor that was driven from the tractor's hydraulic system. The motor drove the PTO shaft, which in turn, since it was transmission driven, ended up driving the transmission at a slow speed useful for certain farming tasks, especially transplanting. With the engine clutch disengaged, the Hydra-Creeper was controlled by a lever and by the PTO shifter rod. The

Hydra-Creeper was made available later in 1954 to the Super A and A-1 family and the new 100 and 200 tractors.

Big Tractors: H, M, 4, 6, and 9

IH's small tractor sales were lagging in the new decade, but the medium and large row-crop tractors and their

Here's a WD-6 plowing somewhere in dairy land. The WD-6s used the same diesel (roughly) as the MD. The start-on gas feature was nice, but the complicated cylinder head had cracking problems. State Historical Society of Wisconsin

standard-tread brothers sold well. Farmall Works had been turning out tractors at full speed since World War II ended in 1945, even with its dependence on material availability and labor strikes (one of which wiped out more than 30,000 potential tractors). The Farmall H and M were the main sellers, but the Farmall Works also produced the 4 and 6 family, which shared a large number of parts with the row crops. Orchard tractor sales were slowing down, as most were discontinued in

1952. The industrial market for wheel tractors was declining in favor of utility tractors and specialized equipment. Still, the Farmall market was great in the early part of the decade.

As the decade wore on, however, the Korean War started to slow tractor production. Material shortages forced substitutions and delayed manufacturing. Marketing analyses predicted that the future was to be somewhat rougher.

A Channel frame Super W-6 with a no. 45 baler near Hinsdale, Illinois. There's an interesting looking hayrack behind the baler. The 45 baler was PTO driven, as opposed to the engine-driven balers in the McCormick line. It was a good match for the Super W-6. State Historical Society of Wisconsin

The tractors now being sold were first produced in 1939, and their designs were dated back before that. By the late 1940s, farmers were asking for several new features. More power was at the top of the list, and more transmission speeds and an independent PTO were close behind. Initially, IH planned an all-new "Super" line of tractors in 1951, at a cost of $20 million in tooling and development costs. An all-new transmission was planned, as well as an improved engine and Touch Control hydraulics (which had been shown on experimental Ms as far back as 1943 and introduced to the public on the "Intermediate M" in 1945).

Production on the new line was delayed, however, and then eliminated. The company decided, instead, to improve the existing tractors in several phases. Larger horsepower was the first major change in production. Increased power required more than just putting in a bigger engine. The engineers had made many changes in the H and M transmissions since 1939 to improve reliability and capacity. Other changes in design and materials improved the tractors further. Preparations for tractors that were even further revised moved into high gear in the late 1940s.

The planning and experimentation finally hit the dealerships in 1952. The Super M (known inside the engineering department as the Stage I Super M) had the new C-264 engine, with a 4-inch stroke and a 5 1/2-inch bore. The new engine was also built in an LPG version for the first time in an International Harvester tractor. The new LPG engine had a different carburetor, radiator outlet pipe, pistons and rings, cranking motor, and electrical cables to handle the new fuel as well as the higher compression ratio that came with it. The diesels of the line were increased to 264 ci.

To handle the increased horsepower, and to prepare for future Stages II, III, and IV, the chassis was changed. Some changes were actually made in late M and W-6 production, while most were made at the Super M and -6 introduction. Changes included a different clutch housing, a rear frame cover that had the left-hand corner cut off, and tapped holes for the old band brake equipment. Covers were omitted. Double disc brakes were used on all Super Ms and -6s.

A few Super Ms, as well as the I-6A industrial tractors, soldiered on with a smaller engine. Industrial modifications of Super Ms received C-248 engines, same as the old M engines, but with new positive exhaust valve rotators and a new flywheel to accommodate the 12-inch clutches fitted into the Super M and Super -6s.

The Super H and Super W-4 were introduced after the Super M and -6. Double disc brakes were used for these tractors as well. The tractors featured a 164-ci engine, replacing the C-152.

Stage II tractors in the Farmall line had live hydraulics. Previously, the H and M tractors had a hydraulic pump mounted in the clutch housing that required the clutch to be engaged for the pump to run. This interfered mightily with things like bucket operations and raising implements at the end of a row. The standard tractors had live hydraulics for quite some time; some orchard tractors quietly received the live hydraulics in 1947. The engines for both standards and Farmalls (essentially the same engines) had all received the modifications necessary to run the Pesco hydraulic pump off the ignition drive in 1950. The W-4 and W-6 received the pumps and valve gear necessary in 1951.

The introduction into the Farmalls was complicated by the tractor's layout and waited for a short time. Both the Super H and Super M received hydraulics after having been sold as Stage I tractors for a time. The addition of live hydraulics involved taking the pump and reservoir out of the clutch housing (thus making room for the addition of the Torque Amplifier later). The Pesco hydraulic pump went to the distributor drive (which of course was unaffected by clutching), while the hydraulic fluid reservoir went under the fuel tank. The battery box, which was under the tank, was moved under the seat. In later Stage II Super H and Super M tractors, and the Super W-6 channel frames, small changes in various parts began to show up in anticipation of future Torque Amplifier and IPTO production.

Major changes took place in the Super -6s in mid-1952. At serial number 3950, the familiar cast front frame of the -6s was replaced by channel frames similar to the Super M. At the same time, changes were made to accommodate LPG equipment. The engines received the same crankcase front covers and engine supports as the Super M, reducing parts counts and production complications there. The chassis changes were more complicated, including of course the new channel frames, but also a new clutch housing construction that was the same as the Super M and moved away from the old standard construction of having the clutch housing bottom half included in the transmission housing, and the top half a separate piece.

Stage III Farmall Super MTAs received the optional Torque Amplifier (located in the clutch housing) and the new transmission that included the optional Independent Power Take Off. In marketing studies conducted in the late 1940s and early 1950s, the new feature farmers most wanted to see was more transmission speeds. Matching the speed of the tractor to what the implement needed for a certain con-

dition could greatly increase productivity. Another goal was power shift, the ability to change speeds in the field doing work without stopping.

Planetary gearing for tractors had received a lot of attention over the years. International Harvester used planetary gearing back in the Mogul 8-16/10-20 and the International 8-16 tractors without power-shift. From 1915 to 1922, Henry Ford had obsessed over planetary gearing in tractors, trying to get the advantages of his Model T transmission into a tractor. IH put planetary steering into the TD-24 in 1947, although it had problems because of a short development time.

In the Super MTA and Super W6-TA, IH used an auxiliary planetary gearset located in the clutch housing to achieve a high-low range powershift. In normal use, the entire unit rotated without a gear reduction. When the operator encountered tough going or wished to reduce speed, a lever on the left

The Super M was essentially a Farmall M with an increased bore engine and some transmission improvements to handle the power. State Historical Society of Wisconsin

The Super WD-9 was the beast of the IH line in the mid-1950s. Intended for heavy tillage, that's just what this tractor is doing. IH preferred that the Super WD-9 use the same implements the W-9 used but pull them faster to avoid stressing the rear end of the tractor. State Historical Society of Wisconsin

side of the tractor was pulled back, operating both the main and TA clutch, which released the unit to use the planetary gears to act as a gear reduction.

The IPTO, also released by IH for the first time in these tractors, used a planetary gearset located at the rear of the tractor in a housing mounted on the back of the transmission case. IH had experimented with independent PTOs since 1900, when a McCormick Automower used the IPTO to great advantage during demonstrations at the World's Fair in France. Experiments continued in the 1930s with electric and front-mounted PTOs. In the early 1940s, IH developed an independent PTO system in a Farmall E, the ancestor of the Farmall C, using a PTO

shaft running directly from the engine to the rear of the tractor. It wasn't manufactured, however, because the E's small size made the price of the system too great. The system had to wait until the H and M were ready for replacement, which was originally scheduled for 1949 but was delayed until 1954.

But the company began preparing for these replacements, and for even more changes coming in the Stage IV tractors, as early as 1952. The transmission was changed and the rear frame was modified to accept the coming two-point hitch. The clutch housing was lengthened 5 inches, which resulted in different hoods, electrical systems, hoses, and other parts. Also necessary were revised front axles for the

The Stage II Super Ms had live hydraulics, with the reservoir located under the fuel tank and the battery moved to under the seat. The tractor would have had more than enough power for the combine. State Historical Society of Wisconsin

high-crop tractors and revised upper bolsters and radiator grilles to handle the hinged cultivators then coming into favor.

The W-9 and WD-9, along with their industrial cousins the I and ID-9, had their production transferred from Milwaukee Works to the Melrose Park industrial power plant in 1948. The next big change in store was the addition of live hydraulics in late 1950 and early 1951. Previously, the agricultural tractors had no hydraulics at all. Hydraulics were being used primarily with big implements. The new hydraulics were not intended for mounted implements because the agricultural 9s never had any; they were intended for the remote operation of implement lifts. The I-9 was never made a Super, although some Super features made it into production. The I-9 ceased production in early 1954.

The decal says Super MD, but the equipment says experimental Super MD-TA. The Torque Amplifier controls and the longer clutch housing are clearly visible. It's getting tested with an H- and M-150 two-furrow disk plow. State Historical Society of Wisconsin

2

1954–1956

Tractors With "Dash"

International Harvester finally stepped away from its old styling, although not too far, in late 1954. Fast Hitch was introduced through the entire size range, except for the large Super WO-9 Series (the only tractors from the old Super series until the 600 replaced them in 1956). Revised hydraulics were used throughout the tractor line, and the 300 series saw the introduction of the Torque Amplifier and independent PTO. Sales continued to decline during the period, although IH maintained its market leadership. Competition grew fiercer as the market for all tractors shrank. IH management refused to accept that the market was permanently shrinking, even though predictions of the shrinkage had been made since the 1940s. The result was large numbers of tractors made with overtime labor, then layoffs as tractors sat on sales lots.

This IH exhibit at the 1955 national plowing contest at Wabash, Indiana, shows a lot of what IH was doing at the time. An IH truck spreading water is on the left, and what looks like a tractor rodeo Fast Hitch demonstration area is on the right. State Historical Society of Wisconsin

It's not an antique tractor show, but a product introduction show for Stockton Works implements and other IH equipment at Riverside, California. California was a major market for IH since the company started in 1902. State Historical Society of Wisconsin

The Farmall Cub received several changes. The most visible change was the restyling, which involved a new hood and fuel tank assembly, new radiator grille and screen, and IH and Farmall Cub emblems instead of the old decals. The changes required the design of a new underhood muffler and exhaust attachment as well. The air cleaner was modified to use a shorter intake air stack, and a new fuel tube was needed to clear the new exhaust.

The International Cub Lo-Boy filled a need in the IH industrial line in 1955. The discontinuance of the I-12 in 1940 left industrial dealers without a small tractor capable of working in the very tight clearances of old factories or working in the nooks and crannies

that sometimes occur even in newer buildings. While Hebard Shop Mules could perform some of those duties, Buda had bought Hebard in 1951, which then was purchased by Allis Chalmers. The Industrial Power Division had experimented with an Industrial C in the late 1940s, but nothing really came of the project. Attention then turned to the Cub. Putting the Cub through roughly the same program as the C and rotating the final drive drop housings, a prototype Cub Lo-Boy was built in 1951.

The new tractor had as standard an underslung exhaust pipe and muffler on the left side of the tractor, again lowering its height. A nonadjustable front axle was used, with tread adjustment made at the

IH held a dealer demonstration at the Riverside in August 1955 that was apparently a little warm. A Cub Lo-Boy used a small wagon to sell Popsicles, but apparently the dry ice didn't last long. D. A. Murray, photographer, State Historical Society of Wisconsin

front and rear wheels. The resulting tractor was 8 feet long, had a turning radius of 8 feet, and a height of 55 inches over the steering wheel. Total ground clearance was 10 3/4 inches under the transmission case. Operating weight listed at 1,640 pounds. The small tractor soon found favor in a wide variety of operations where small size and low center of gravity were critical. Many were bought by state highway departments for roadside mowing. A feature that started showing up was rear duals—not for the increased traction, but because it allowed the tractor to work on increased slopes.

In the early years of International Cub Lo-Boy production, the Lo-Boy name was only used in the United States and Canada. Outside the United States, the name was "McCormick International Cub Special." "Special" decals were placed on the sides of the

radiator screen, and the "Lo-Boy" nameplate was omitted. The reason for the nameplate change was probably overseas government testing and licensing. A new name of "Lo-Boy" would have meant a separate testing and licensing procedure, while calling it a "special" meant that the new tractor qualified for sale under the original Farmall Cub license.

The 100 and 200

A mild restyling and new hydraulic systems were in store for late 1954. The major changes on the 100 and 200 chassis were new radiator grilles, hoods, and nameplates instead of decals to identify model and make. Fast Hitch, available on the Super C since 1953, was extended to the 100 and the Cub, the smaller tractors getting the one-point Fast Hitch. In the case of the Cub and 100, the Fast Hitch worked with the old Touch

The Cub Lo-Boy was introduced in 1955. Based on the Cub tractor, the Lo-Boy was intended for industrial uses, including roadside mowing and maintenance. The Farmall Cub of this era had identical styling. State Historical Society of Wisconsin

Control hydraulics. Early 100s had some problems with durability in the areas where the hitch mounted, but this was soon corrected.

Both the 100 and 200 used a slightly revised (and slightly different between them) C-123 engine. The 100 engine ran at 1,400 rpm, while the 200 engine ran at 1,650.

Farm Tractor Decision 1879 eliminated the International 100. Industrial tractor features could be ordered with the Farmall 100, including the foot accelerator, heavy-duty front axle, front lamp bracket, industrial tires, and the deduct for Touch Control hydraulics. Some customers liked to have a separate tractor, however, so IH later reinstated the I-100. The

Electralls

International Harvester and General Electric combined efforts in the 1950s to research the additional uses that electricity could have on the farm. One of the products that resulted was the Electrall. The Electrall was a small generator that could be mounted on the clutch housing and driven by a belt off of the IPTO drive gear of the tractor, or driven by the PTO and mounted on a small wagon or a Fast Hitch mounting. The electricity could be used as either backup for the normal power grid or to drive small power tools around the farm far from an outlet. Beyond this, IH examined several other ideas.

One major push was to use the Electrall as a replacement for the rotating shaft of the PTO, instead running cables between implement and tractor. A combine and hay baler were marketed briefly using these ideas. Another

The Farmall 400 in the foreground is an Electrall demonstrator. The Electrall unit is painted silver, as is the electric motor on the hay baler in the back. An electric cable eliminated the PTO shaft, but a small capacity was a problem. State Historical Society of Wisconsin

major thrust was to use electricity in crop cultivation, using ultraviolet light or electrical arcs to kill weeds.

The Super MTA and Super W6-TA had Electrall packages released in mid-1955. The differences from the 400 Series packages were mainly cables, switch boxes, and fuel pipes.

The Electrall was an interesting idea, but the idea failed to sell well. Either the generator was too small (to provide backup power for a farm), too inefficient (the belt drive had a low mechanical efficiency, leading back to the too small, and it was wasteful), or too big (running a big tractor engine was an expensive way to drive small power tools). After selling some units in the mid-1950s, IH converted the generators to the configuration that had the best chance of selling (the trail behind units) and closed out the line.

The 200 was a good all-around tractor. Here's one with a somewhat rare IH loader, loading what looks like feed or lime into an IH truck at the Hinsdale Farm. The radiator guard is a bit unusual. State Historical Society of Wisconsin

new International 100 was actually a Farmall 100 with an International nameplate. Why? Some customers wanted tractors known as Internationals, rather than Farmalls.

The 300 and 400

The 300s and 400s saw more change than the smaller tractors. The big news was the new 300 Utility. This tractor was known throughout development as the "International Utility Tractor" or the "International All-Duty," but was renamed shortly before production. A tractor based on the Ford 8N replaced the Super W-4

(in fact, an 8N was disassembled at Hinsdale, Illinois, during the engineering process, a frequent practice for tractor engineering programs for all companies). The tractor featured a lower profile for use in buildings and other low clearances (such as orchards), while being made more amenable to loaders. The tractors found a ready market among both farm and industrial markets. Originally known as the "International 300" when released, the name was changed to "International 300 Utility" in mid-1955.

The International 400 bore some resemblance to the International 300, but in fact it was close kin to

Although IH's Utility tractor line was more commonly associated with loaders, here's an unadorned tractor pulling a four-row corn planter in the field. The 300 Utilities were aimed at the market pioneered by Ford-Ferguson's 9N. State Historical Society of Wisconsin

the Super W6-TA. Like the 300, the name was changed in May or June 1955, but the 400 became the International W-400.

The Farmall and International 300 received the new C-169 engine. This engine had more power than the C-164 of the Super H, produced from an engine that had a 1/16-inch larger bore than the C-164's 3 inches. Rpms were raised from 1,650 to 1,750 in the International 300 and some 100s, while some other International 100s were rated at 2,000 rpm. A new carburetor was used to supply the extra fuel needed.

The 300s were available in LPG, kerosene-distillate, and gasoline versions. The Farmall 300 was available in the high-crop version whose components were little changed from those of the HV.

The Farmall 400 had slightly more horsepower than the MTA. Compression ratios were raised slightly to 6.3:1 (gasoline version), and a new distributor assembly was used. Top engine rpm was dropped to 1,450 from 1,600, a popular selling point with salesmen who could point to lower wear and stresses. The Farmall 400 was available in

An International 300 Utility playing in the dirt at a Hinsdale Allied equipment show. IH passed out snazzy red cowboy hats to dealers at the shows, while the gray-and-white shirts were standard uniforms for service and dealership personnel. State Historical Society of Wisconsin

kerosene-distillate, gasoline, LPG, and diesel versions, and it was available in standard and high-crop versions. It also served as the power and chassis of high- and low-drum cotton pickers.

The big Farmalls both received Fast Hitch for the first time, as well as a more advanced hydraulic system with integral lift system. The actual hitch points were larger than on the Super C or 200,

The 300, with its live PTO and hydraulics, was an excellent choice to power a pickup, self-tying hay baler. If an area of heavy hay threatened to plug up the baler, the driver could step on the clutch to stop forward movement, while the PTO kept moving to bale through the heavy spot. These balers took a lot of work out of baling, although plenty remained. State Historical Society of Wisconsin

although the smaller point implements could still be used with a special adapter. Fast Hitch was limited to tractors with two- or three-valve Hydra-Touch hydraulic systems.

The Farmall 300 received as optional the Torque Amplifier and IPTO, as did the 300 Utility. The two features, first brought to production on the Super MTA and Super W6-TA, produced a small tractor that was very full featured. In fact, the 300 and 400 were originally known as the Super H and Super M Stage IV.

Sheet metal was changed extensively. The hood had three sections, a left and right rear section and a front section. Instead of the hood line blending into the fuel tank like earlier tractors, the hood extended back into an instrument panel/reservoir housing, which also housed the hydraulic valves. The instrument panel housed the ignition and starting switch,

instrument panel lights, the battery charge indicator, oil pressure gauge, and heat indicator all into one location, rather than spread out all over the tractor, as on the earlier H, and Ms. In addition, a cigar lighter was added to the panel. Hydraulic levers were located on the right side of the panel and were now exclusively live hydraulics, rather than optional. Multiple hydraulic valves were used for single- or double-acting cylinders.

The International 300 Utility received a new special attachment in early 1955 that would rapidly become a favorite, especially for loader tractors: power steering. A Ross integral type steering unit was used. Only tractors fitted with Hydra-Touch (either one, two, or three valves) could be fitted with the new attachment, as hydraulics were needed to power the Ross unit. On the Utility, factory or field installation was possible. The International 400 had power steering

The Farmall 400 shows off its clean lines. Visible is the revised operator's position with a new instrument panel and hydraulic levers. Hydraulic lines have been rerouted to improve appearance as well. The disc is Fast Hitch mounted. State Historical Society of Wisconsin

as well from the beginning of production but used a Monroe integral unit with an Eaton hydraulic pump working off the fan belt.

Power steering attachments for the Farmall 300 and 400 series tractors became available in early 1956. Behlen hydraulic power boosters were assembled as an integral part of the steering shaft. As mentioned above, the system could only be used on tractors with Hydra-Touch hydraulic systems. Other parts necessary were new regulators, flow valves, tubes, and attaching parts. The attachments were factory-only when released.

The low-profile International 300 Utility was well suited for orchard work. A new lower seat, designed specifically for orchard work was authorized in 1956. The seat was taken from the Farmall 100. Orchard fenders were available as a parts attachment for field installation.

The Super WD-9 and WR-9S

The Super WD and WDR-9 were the last of the letter-series tractors to remain in production. The author doesn't know why the 600 took so long to release, but the Super WD-9 (and the WR-9S, which had the

Tractors with factory LP equipment had been available from IH since the advent of the Super M. This LPG Farmall 400 is picking corn with a 21 Corn Snapper. State Historical Society of Wisconsin

chassis improvements of the Super WDs with the older W-9 engine) continued to soldier on until 1956. The rear frames were limited in how much horsepower could be put through them, and possibly this problem was more difficult to work through than in the smaller tractors.

The Super WDs had a lot of chassis improvements. Strengthened differentials, double disc brakes, electrical parts, nameplates, and fastening screws were used, as well as a new radiator grille to accommodate an increased capacity radiator. The rear frame was updated, as well as new gearshift rails and other parts.

The WR-9S was approved for production in March 1954. The same chassis improvements made in the Super WDs were made in the WR-9S, but the old C-335 engine was unchanged.

The Super WDs received power steering in late 1954. An integral linkage type was used with a Monroe hydraulic cylinder and integral valve and an Eaton hydraulic pump driven by the fan belt. If the tractor to be fitted did not have a hydraulic system, the normal reservoir was installed as part of the steering system. If the tractor had a hydraulic system, the existing reservoir was used.

An Allied equipment show at Hinsdale, probably in 1955. The new Cub Lo-Boys and International 300 Utilities were prominent, but an International 400 fitted with an unusual piece of lifting equipment and a front blade was also shown. State Historical Society of Wisconsin

The 600 didn't replace the Super WD-9 until 1956. The heavy tractor had the same styling as the rest of the Hundred Series Tractors, but still had the old start-on gas features (and problems) of the old WD-9s. Today, these are rare tractors. State Historical Society of Wisconsin

The 600

The 600 was not authorized for production until August 31, 1956, more than two years after its 100 series siblings hit the production floor. The new tractors featured several improvements, including an increase in the steering ratio and the height of the steering wheel, a new positive engagement starter to handle the larger engines, new operator platforms and rear fenders, and a hydraulic swinging seat. Styling was revamped with a new radiator grille, hood, and instrument panel. The throttle control lever was now lubricated, a weather cap was fitted for the exhaust pipe, and new, larger lights were used.

The 600 saw new C-350 gas engines released, a recognition that the tractors could handle more horsepower through the transmissions and rear ends. A new D-350 diesel was also available that had an adjustable jet venturi for the gasoline starting system to help with cold starting.

The 600s were the first International Harvester tractors available from the start of production with hydraulics power steering. The system used many parts available for Super WD and WDR-9 special attachments, but it had new regulators, valve assemblies and covers, and hoses. A "Power Steering" nameplate was used when the attachment was used on a tractor. The power steering attachment could be fitted either at the factory or in the field.

3

1956–1958

Two-Tone Tractors

International Harvester tractors received a little make-over in 1956. Tractors from other companies displayed two-tone paint jobs at the 1956 Pennsylvania Road Show, a sales convention for road-building equipment. IH followed suit, creating a white decal to go under the ID name on the hood, the radiator grille was painted white. Not much else changed from the previous 100 series, other than the gradual improvements that took place regardless of model changes.

The Cub and Cub Lo-Boy didn't change names or major mechanical features for the 1957 model changes. The only thing that changed was the new white paint on the radiator grille, the new white hood sheet nameplate background decal, and the IH hood emblem changed the black background to a new Harvester Red background.

By the 1956 introduction of the 50 and 30 series tractors, the power hunger of American farms was demanding big tractors. The Farmall 450s were the popular tractors of the era for IH, although the 650s were selling their share as well. State Historical Society of Wisconsin

41

The 130s were the descendants of the 100s, themselves descended originally from the Farmall A. The 130 and 130 High Crop received the increased horsepower C-123 engine that operated at 1,800 rpm instead of the 1,650 of the older tractors. The crankcase, sleeves, valves, and governor received some updates. A new manifold was used, and new carburetors from Zenith and Carter were used. New IH distributors were designed to give maximum advance at 1,800 rpm.

Other parts were updated to handle the new speeds and to increase part commonality with the Farmall 230s. A new air cleaner, carburetor, and rear lamp supports taken from the 300/400 series tractors (again increasing commonality) were used. The rear frame of the tractor was revised to add a pad for the new Fast Hitch used on the 230 (which shared the same rear frame assembly as the 130). The paint scheme and white nameplate decal were the extent of the other major changes. Tractor speeds were increased due to the increased engine rpm.

The Farmall 230 was also a 200 with some more extensive revisions than its little brother. The increased horsepower C-123 was there similar to the 130, but a new single-valve Hydra-Touch hydraulic system was used, as well as the new weight-transfer, articulated-linkage Fast Hitch. A two-valve Hydra-Touch system and a rear hydraulic manifold were available as a special attachment. Weight transfer allowed the draft of the implement to be transferred as downward force to the rear traction wheels, giving additional traction, critical in small tractors.

Left: Led by the Cub Lo-Boy, the IH tractors built between 1956 and 1958 follow along. The two-tone color scheme featured a painted white radiator and was inspired by a certain other company at the 1956 Pennsylvania Road Show. State Historical Society of Wisconsin

Ford-Ferguson had introduced this feature to America in the 9N in 1939, but patents and some nasty lawsuits scared many other manufacturers out of weight transfer until the mid-1950s. After the hydraulics, which introduced weight transfer into IH's small tractors for the first time, the major changes were paint and decals. A new toolbox and seat assembly were fitted to eliminate provisions for the old rockshaft bearings and other older parts no longer used on the new tractor. Tractor speeds were also increased by the higher rpm engine.

The 330 was a tractor that happened by chance. The original schedule for the production of new 40 and 60 series tractors was fall 1956 for 1957 production. The new lines were delayed by a variety of problems, however, mainly financial. The engine for the new 340 was tooled up and ready to produce. What IH did was take the new C-135 engine and mate it with the 350 basic chassis, although some 340 parts were used there as well. The resulting tractor was called the 330, reflecting both the chassis and the slightly smaller engine.

The 350

The changes in the new 350 line foreshadowed many events to come. The chassis of the 350s, both Farmalls and Utilities, saw the new weight transfer Fast Hitch and new push-button starting (replacing the turnkey of the 100s), as well as the two-tone paint, hood sheet decal, and new serial number plates. The gas tractors received the new C-175 increased horsepower engine. The engine bore was increased 1/16 inch over the C-169 used in the 100s by using new thin-wall cylinder sleeves and larger pistons and rings.

The diesel-powered tractors were where new ground was covered. IH went outside the company to purchase direct-starting diesels from Continental Motors. Although IH had produced small

The 130 was an updated 100. Here's a great view of the one-point Fast Hitch, which of course was exclusive to the Cub and 130. The plow is a 1-F-11 one-bottom, two-way plow. State Historical Society of Wisconsin

direct-starting diesels in Germany since 1950, and had recently put similar engines into production in England, domestic IH engines were not ready for production. The decision authorizing the new Continentals calls the tractors "Direct Starting Diesel 350" leaving little doubt which new feature the engineering and sales departments desired. The GD-193 engine was selected, which was a four-cylinder, 3 3/4x4 3/8 bore and stroke operating at 1,750 rpm for the Farmalls and 2,000 rpm for the Utilities.

The Continentals had a reputation of being hard to start, but soon, new IH diesel engines would come into U.S. production.

Both diesel and gas utilities were offered from the start of production in an orchard version (both for factory and field application) using parts that were used in a field attachment for 300 Utilities. The 350s and 350Ds were also built in Wheatland versions that had an increased ground clearance heavy-duty front axle (similar to the Hi-Utilities), a new platform at

continued on page 50

Above: *This 230 is pulling a no. 43 disc harrow built by IH Stockton Works in California. The 230 descended from the Farmall C line.* D. A. Murray, photographer, State Historical Society of Wisconsin

Next Page: *With the small tractors close to the camera, the Farmall family is on the left with the Cub, 130, 230, 350, and 450. On the right is the Cub Lo-boy, International 130, the International 300 Utility, the W-450, and the 650. The family likeness is very apparent, just what the sales department likes.* State Historical Society of Wisconsin

The Rest of the Company

International Harvester was never just about tractors. The company manufactured many different product lines on most of the continents during the 1950s, including:

• Farm equipment: IH was the first of the "full-line" farm equipment companies, providing virtually every kind of equipment the average farmer needed, including power (both tractor and power unit), tillage, forage, harvesting, and material handling equipment. IH was forever looking for more

to produce as well. The company produced quite a bit of specialty equipment, including cotton, cane, sugar beet, and market garden equipment.

• Construction: IH got into the construction and industrial power business from the start of tractor production, but seriously got into industrial power in the early 1920s with the 10-20 Industrial, and into the construction business in the mid-1930s with larger crawler tractors. By the 1950s, IH was committed to the construction equipment business. It had devoted

Although when IH was founded the focus was solely on farm equipment, by 1908 IH was producing trucks, and it never stopped. Trucks were, of course, very popular and necessary for American farmers. This L-120 truck is getting really, really loaded with pumpkins. State Historical Society of Wisconsin

IH offered quite a line of industrial and light crawler equipment in the late 1950s and early 1960s. This industrial dealer is selling a Canadian-built T-4 crawler, a T-340 with an attractively painted four-in-one bucket, a 330 Utility with a dozer blade, what looks like a 40 series utility tractor under a loader bucket, and a British-built B-275 or B-250. The sun never set on IH.
State Historical Society of Wisconsin

several factories and a lot of capital to it; however, the IH Caterpillar met stiff competition that it was never able to overcome. Construction and industrial products included crawler and wheel tractors, scrappers, allied equipment, Payhauler dump trucks, and an agreement with Frank Hough Inc. that IH eventually turned into a purchase, to produce Payloader four-wheel-drive bucket loaders.

• Trucks: IH was the market leader in heavy trucks by the 1950s and did well in the light truck market. The company had produced trucks since 1907. The trucks were engineered originally by Ed Johnston, designer of the McCormick Automower, the Mogul line of tractors, and engineer of many other things around IH.

• Refrigeration: Born out of its dairy equipment line, IH began producing limited refrigeration equipment in the late 1930s. By the early 1950s, the line had grown to include both household refrigeration and freezers. The company had trouble trying to get into the urban retail market, however. There were few established dealers, and money was short, so IH sold the line in the mid-1950s.

• Military: Like many companies during the Cold War, IH had military contracts, although it wasn't as successful as others. IH sold wheel tractors and equipment, crawler tractors and equipment, armored personnel carriers, rifles, trucks, and other items to the military.

LOW PROFILE

E-20

The 330 Utility was built from 340 engines and other parts and 350 chassis parts when the 340 was ready for production before the rest of the line. The resemblance to the 350 Utility is nearly identical. State Historical Society of Wisconsin

Continued from page 44

the top of the main frame cover similar to that of the International W-450, new fenders combining the crown of the W-450 with new side sheets, and new "Wheatland" decals. Fast Hitches couldn't be used with Wheatlands, and revised IPTOs, PTOs, and lighting attachments had to be designed to clear the new platforms and fenders. The first 350 Wheatlands, both diesel and carbureted, were built on March 4, 1957.

The Utilities also saw some new applications in specialty crops. Both diesel and carbureted versions

were produced with a "Hi-Clear" attachment for shade tobacco producers. The tractors featured Farmall 350 rear axles, wheels, and tire equipment (giving adjustable widths). Modified front-axle extensions and steering knuckles gave 5 inches of additional crop clearance. Different drive bevel gears yielded speeds the same as the regular Utilities, even with the larger rear tires. "Hi-Clear" nameplates were used instead of the "Utility" nameplates. There was some confusion between the Utility Hi-Clears and the Farmall Hi-Clears, so later in 1957, the names were changed to

This is a pretty well-equipped farmer. A TD-6 crawler is grubbing out brush, a Farmall 350 is cultivating some very young plants, and, of course, a lovely woman is bringing out a meal in a very pink IH A series pickup. State Historical Society of Wisconsin

An updated view has a Farmall 350 pulling a later hay baler than the 300 photo. The field is in the contoured farming area of the IH Farm in Hinsdale, Illinois. IH was a major proponent of conservation farming since at least the 1930s. The IH Farm acted as a demonstration area, even though it was pretty flat. State Historical Society of Wisconsin

"Hi-Utility." With the change in name, the restriction on sales to only shade tobacco producers was lifted.

The Farmall 450 and W-450 saw a change to push-button starting, new C-281 and D-281 engines with increased horsepower, and the introduction of the new weight-transfer Fast Hitch, which was helpful in heavy-traction situations. The new engines had a 1/8-inch increased bore over the C-264 engines used in the 400s. The extra bore was achieved by the use of new thin-wall cylinder sleeves in the old block. The two-tone paint and new white hood sheet nameplate decal matched the rest of the line. The 450s retained the start-on gas diesels and were, of course, also available with LPG fuel equipment as well. The

The diesel 450s were the last of the start-on gas IH diesels, along with the diesel 650s. A Continental diesel engine was being used in the 350s. This was all replaced by direct-start, six-cylinder IH diesels in 1958. State Historical Society of Wisconsin

This Farmall 400 is fitted with frame weights and is pulling a 4-F-43 Fast Hitch four-bottom plow. Visible is the control panel that placed the gauges all in one place, rather than all over the tractor as before. Although the hydraulic levers are now small and in one place, that's still a long IPTO lever on the right side of the tractor. State Historical Society of Wisconsin

Farmall 450s were also available in high-crop versions. The 450s were the real strength of IH's farm tractor line sales as farms got larger and numbers got smaller; however, the increased horsepower started to result in an increased rate of rear-end failures, which had plagued the larger IH tractors since at least the Super Series. This problem would soon explode in later tractors.

Although IH had used 12-volt electrical systems since 1941 for its diesel tractors, and since the early 1950s on its LPG tractors, the company finally got around to replacing the old 6-volt systems on the oth-

er carbureted tractors in 1957. The 450s received the welcome change, using many parts from the diesels and LPGs, but with a new cranking motor and ventilated generators. The battery ignition distributor and coil remained 6-volt, but with a resistor that cut out to allow a full 12 volts to the coil during cranking.

The 650

The switch from the short-lived and apparently somewhat troublesome International 600 to the 650 involved quite a few changes, unlike most of IH's American product changeovers of this time. A new

This is the International 650 with LPG, probably a prototype. LPG enjoyed a period of popularity especially in the large tractors, but could not withstand the diesel onslaught that began (at least for IH) with the 460/560 tractors with direct starting. This tractor is a rare find today. State Historical Society of Wisconsin

C-350 gas engine and a new D-350 diesel increased horsepower. New fenders increased tire coverage and improved appearance. The brake locking mechanisms were revised, and new clutch pedals and operating rods were used to reduce clutch pedal effort. The paint and decals were changed, of course, and the IH hood emblem background was changed to red instead of black.

1958–1960
More Power

The Cubs

In the last years of the 1950s, the International Harvester Cubs were influenced by the new design concepts of Raymond Loewy, the independent industrial design consultant who styled the 1939 tractor. The radiator grille and grille supports were the main changes. A new friction-type governor control was used, and 12-volt electrical systems finally meant the end of the somewhat despised, often cursed, and usually converted 6-volt systems, an especially welcome change in the colder regions of the country.

The 140

The 140 and 140 High Clearance were authorized in late 1956 for production in November 1957. Unfortunately, the production prediction was optimistic by

The 1958 product introduction show at Hinsdale, Illinois, was an extremely successful event for IH just when it needed it. The show was visited by twice the number of dealers anticipated, and 20,000 tractors were sold in two weeks. Product reliability put a damper on the results. State Historical Society of Wisconsin

57

The Farmall Cub for 1958 featured a grille with bars and a new model symbol to match the rest of the new IH tractor family. This Cub is in use in either a market garden, or else what may be just a large home garden. Of course, hired men never bring home the boss' tractor to put in a few tomatoes. State Historical Society of Wisconsin

more than six months. The new C-123 engines in the tractors used a single belt to drive the water pump, fan, and generator, eliminating a vestige of the old thermosyphon system of the C-113-powered model As. New radiator grilles and supports helped update the styling, and a modern 12-volt electrical system was installed. Various other small changes, including new model symbols matching the larger tractors of the line,

were also fitted. A nameplate attachment was available for customers who wanted "International" tractors instead of "Farmalls," but the content of the package was two "International" nameplates, period.

The 240

The 240 was essentially a 230 with improved hydraulics (the "Micro-Set Tel-A-Depth" system). The seat and rear platform were renovated, and, of course, new sheet metal was added with the new Raymond Loewy styling. Two- or three-point hitches were available. A new rear transmission casing was used. The 240 was made in a Farmall, International Utility, and industrial version.

An increased-clearance, wide front axle was available for the 240 in early 1959. The attachment used new steering knuckle assemblies and axle extension assemblies to increase clearance from 17.0 inches to 20.2 inches. The axles were available as either factory-installed attachments or field-installed parts assemblies in conjunction with the sale of larger rear wheels and a different hitch in one package.

The 340

The 340 was a new small tractor that had many features of larger tractors. TA and IPTO were built into a smaller tractor that filled a gap between the 240 and the 460.

Cubs and Cub Lo-Boys proved very popular in the industrial grounds maintenance and industrial tractor market, where their small size and versatility made groundskeepers happy. This Lo-Boy has a belly-mount mower and a Wayne loader attachment. In the background, dinosaurs with doctorates are making new oils for your DeSoto. State Historical Society of Wisconsin

This photograph, taken in the early 1960s, shows a fleet of orange 340s and Cub Lo-Boys. IH painted them any color the customer wanted. Notice the dual rear wheels on the Lo-Boys (which added more stability on hillsides). State Historical Society of Wisconsin

New clutch housings and rear frames were used. Two different hydraulic systems were available. One was similar to the old touch control system that had a reservoir and used a pump driven from the camshaft gear. The other used a pump that was fully enclosed on the clutch housing and used the housing and the rear frame as the fluid reservoir. Two- or three-point hitches were available. Twelve-volt electrical systems were standard. The fenders gave extended coverage of tires. The International 340 had a new wide front axle, with manual or power steering, while Farmall 340s had a tricycle front axle and manual steering. An industrial version was available as well.

Cub Lo-Boys were soon painted in yellow after IH made it a no cost option in the late 1950s. These post-1958 Lo-Boys are at work in a cemetery. State Historical Society of Wisconsin

The 340 used the same engine as the 330. Orchard attachments for the I-340 were authorized in June 1959. In appearance, the attachments were very similar to the I-350 attachments. The orchard attachments could be added both at the factory and in the field. The same attachments were used on the International 460 and 460D.

Diesel 340s were authorized in late December 1959, although final authorization had to wait until early 1960, with production taking place even later. A new D-166 direct-start engine with a 3 11/16-inch bore and a 3 7/8-inch stroke was used. The engine had a higher horsepower than the gas engine,

These International 140s have been specially fitted out for the Missouri Highway Department. The shiny canisters under the seats are water coolers. State Historical Society of Wisconsin

Utility 240s were most often found with a loader or an attached mower, but here a "clean" 240 is planting corn. When not covered with equipment, the Utility 240 was quite an attractive tractor. State Historical Society of Wisconsin

so differentials from the 460 series were used, along with 460 brakes, a new larger radiator, new sheet metal to clear the engine, new engine mountings, a new fuel tank, 350 diesel air cleaners, and the I-460D battery box. The diesels were made available both in the Farmall and International versions.

The 460 and 560

The Farmall and International 460 and 560 were essentially beefed-up 350s and 450s, with new six-cylinder engines brought over from the truck division. The diesel versions finally corrected a major failing of IH: It finally introduced direct starting, as opposed to the

start-on earlier gas engines. The gas engines had problems due to their complexity, mainly cylinder heads that cracked often. The new engines were simpler, more reliable (at least over the previous diesels), and more powerful, although the 460 developed a reputation for being more difficult to start in winter.

Originally known as the 360 and 460, the tractors were renumbered to 460 and 560 to reflect the additional horsepower; however, the extra horsepower was sent through the old H and M transmission with Torque Amplifier. The design had been considered to be running near horsepower capacity in 1939. Now, thanks to induction and other hardening of gears,

IH played a major role in helping evolve the 4-H clubs in the United States, and here a young member is mowing with a Farmall 240. The 240s were built only for a short time before being replaced by the 404. They are among the most collectable of the 1958 to 1963 tractors. State Historical Society of Wisconsin

new machining methods, and new advanced gear shapes, the revised H and M transmissions were almost capable of transmitting all that new torque from the six-cylinder engines.

The 460 featured C-221 and D-236 engines, while the 560s featured C-263 and D-282 engines, originally from IH's truck division. The carbureted versions were available in LPG and kerosene/distillate versions. Both tractors featured extensive revisions in the chassis. New radiator grilles had horizontal cross-bars and perforated, new-contour, upper sections. The hoods were made in upper and lower pieces,

matching the new contour in the grille and using the two-tone paint introduced in earlier tractors. The air cleaner intake was located in front of the radiator. Twelve-volt electrical systems were used, critical in the larger tractors. New fenders were used that gave welcome coverage of the tires.

Steering and hydraulics were in for even more extensive changes on the 460s and 560s. The rear frames and clutch housings were modified to incorporate a lube filter. The cast-iron housings became the hydraulic reservoir, using Touch Control hydraulic fluid with Torque Amplifier additives as

Here's the same farm kid with a Farmall 340. The 340 is another desirable tractor in today's collectible market, and they're just plain neat. Although Fast Hitch was standard, IH began to offer three-point hitches in this time period. State Historical Society of Wisconsin

both the transmission lubrication fluid and the hydraulic fluid. The hydraulic pump itself was relocated from the ignition drive back to the clutch housing. The pump was driven by the IPTO drive gear, which of course was powered directly from the engine.

Power or manual steering was available. The power steering was incorporated into the upper bolster for the first time. The manual used the same bolster

but different internals. The International 460s had to have a new front axle designed that would fit under the six-cylinder engine.

A Hi-Utility attachment was made for the International 460 family to succeed the International 350

Right: The 340 Utilities, both red and yellow, made it into the growing construction market. This one is being used as a rough terrain forklift. State Historical Society of Wisconsin

The 340 grove tractor was obviously aimed at the citrus market (note the orange trees behind it). The 340 groves are rare, attractive, and in demand today, along with the rest of the 340 series. The company also produced 460 groves that are similar in appearance. State Historical Society of Wisconsin

Hi-Utility. The attachment on the 460 increased ground clearance 4.3 inches by using the Farmall 460 rear axles and tire equipment and modified front axles and knuckles. The tractor speeds were the same as the Farmall 460, obtained by using Farmall 460 drive bevels and pinion shafts. Fast Hitches could not be used with the Hi-Utilities, but Farmall 460 fixed drawbars could.

Wheatland attachments were also offered on the International 460 (including the LPG) and 460D. Problems were encountered in development, but were ironed out by late November 1958. There were problems with fitting two-point or three-point hitches, but the new attachments could be used with either. IH's original attachment also included a special IPTO to clear the platforms, but the revised attachment could use the standard IPTO. The attachments included new fenders that incorporated the I-560 fender crown, new operator platforms, and the Wheatland symbol plates.

Orchard attachments for the International 460 and 460D (and 340) were authorized in June 1959. In appearance, the attachments were very similar to the I-350 attachments. The orchard attachments could be added both at the factory and in the field.

The problems that the 460 and 560 programs ran into are legendary. IH did a lot of things right with the tractors, which only made problems worse.

The changeover from the old tractor models to the new tractor models at Farmall Works was pain free, requiring only three weeks to go to full production. IH presented the tractors at a very successful dealer introduction at Hinsdale in 1958. The first dealers at the two-week show quickly spread the word about the new tractors, so that by the end of the program, twice the number of dealers had seen the show than had been originally estimated. IH sold 20,000 tractors to those dealers, and they were impressed by the new engines and appearance. It looked as if IH had a major hit on its hands. Tractors flowed quickly to

This is a shot of an experimental Farmall 400 in June 1956. As you can see, the styling (by Raymond Loewy) is set, although there are a variety of other changes to be made around the front bolster. The tractor would go through two more name changes: to the 460, and then to the Farmall 560. State Historical Society of Wisconsin

The 460 was a direct descendent of the Farmall H, but with dramatically more power (Try pulling that disc with an H and you'll soon find out what I mean!). At first the chassis couldn't keep up with the engine, but IH spared no effort in fixing them. State Historical Society of Wisconsin

IH's decision to paint its industrial and crawler tractors yellow at no extra charge in the 1950s soon meant that many yellow tractors were going out the door. Although not commonly thought of as an industrial tractor, this yellow 460 Utility seems to be handling these parts at a substation quite nicely. State Historical Society of Wisconsin

This 460 Utility has an unusual front-mounted forklift, a rear carrier, and a modified air cleaner for use in an apple orchard. Somewhere, there's a good find for a collector. State Historical Society of Wisconsin

customers, who were eager to put the new beasts to work.

Unfortunately, IH had waited too long to introduce new tractors, or perhaps not long enough. Severe financial conditions had forced IH to cut back on its engineering budgets in 1957, basically eliminating advance engineering. Outgoing President John McCaffrey noted in May 1958, that the tractors had not yet been tested, even though they were due to be sold in September. Upper management knew about the problem, but apparently did nothing. Later, engineers were blamed.

The first tractors to be put to work were largely located in the Southwest and West. There, listed land gave more tire-to-soil contact, reducing slippage and increasing torque loads. Soon, tractors in the listed territories began to fail. While in some parts of the country, failure rates were about normal, in other parts of the country failure rates reached and sometimes exceeded 10 percent. Soon, differentials, bull pinions, and crankshafts began to fail. Because the regions where the problems were greatest were the regions where farming was seasonally active, it soon

Farmall 460s were purchased by several county highway departments. This one has a wide front and a two-tone paint job featuring orange. The red of the model symbol sticks out a bit. Other highway department 460s have been seen painted all orange. State Historical Society of Wisconsin

The 560 Standard is introduced at the 1958 Hinsdale show. Using a large number of Farmall 560 parts, the 560 Standard was produced in far fewer numbers. State Historical Society of Wisconsin

looked like IH had a disaster on its hands. Management reacted strongly to the problems, offering a program to fix the problems that flared up first, such as gearing. Tents were set up, and a crash program to fix the first problem was put into motion. After the first program, however, a second round of bearing problems flared up as more northern farmers began their spring work and required a major revision to the fix program. Although IH's competitors suffered their own disasters, some even worse than the 460/560 problems, the reactions by IH management to fix the problems drew a lot of attention fast. The competition was only too happy to help point fingers, while hiding their own failures.

The 660

The large 660 standard tractor also encountered major problems in early production tractors. The tractor was intended for drawbar work and for mounting large commercial equipment. It was all new, inheriting nothing from the 650.

The tractor nearest to the camera is a 560 LP, followed by a straight Farmall 560, a Farmall 460 LPG, a Farmall 460, and a few other unidentified tractors. You can see that the dealers were paying close attention and orders would soon follow. State Historical Society of Wisconsin

Both engine and chassis were based on the International 560. A planetary-type rear axle was used, and a clutch pedal that also operated the TA was used. A hand clutch attachment that also operated the TA was available. The front axle was a 5-inch solid bar with fixed tread. The grille was modified to give a larger appearance than the 560 by adding a cast spacer with the same front design as the top grille (the spacer also acted as a front weight).

The carbureted engine was also similar to the 560 engine, except that the engine ran at 2,400 rpm. To feed the engine a new carburetor was used, and a new distributor able to operate the engine at the higher rpm was used. Other changes included the torsional vibration damper,

Saltillo Works in Mexico wasn't assembling tractors yet, but it was making implements and attachments. The 460 and 560 High Crops had some problems with the Fast Hitch attachments holding up in cane operations, and apparently the Mexican engineering department designed a possible answer. The ME-34-F2 hitch is shown here. State Historical Society of Wisconsin

valves, a different fan pulley, and a new governor spring. Similar changes were made to the diesel. An LPG version of the 660 was also made using many 560 parts, but with different plumbing, fuel tank supports, and radiator support assemblies.

A full coverage fender attachment was authorized in late December 1959 and entered production December 7 of that year. The attachment yielded an extra 9 inches of coverage by using new fenders and fender support assemblies, and it required new rear light supports.

Problems encountered with tractors in the field were fierce. Major problems were encountered with the diesel engines that eventually required new pistons, sleeves, crankshafts, and an inspection of most of the rest of the engine. Chassis were fixed with new transmission mainshaft and bull pinion bearings, TA

Under the cloud of impressed looking IH dealer personnel is the 660 diesel. The 660 replaced the 650, but was in fact based on the 560 Standard tractor. Intended for high horsepower applications in small grain farming, the 660s developed a rash of problems in the field. State Historical Society of Wisconsin

modifications, clutch modifications, new planet hubs, and a variety of other fixes.

Reports from the field to headquarters and letters from customers indicated that the tractor performed excellently—when it performed. Reliability was poor. Finally, in September 1960, the company recalled all new and unused tractors below serial number 4256, built on July 18, 1960, that were still in company or dealer inventories. The tractors were returned to Farmall Works and disassembled. Usable components were used on the assembly line for new tractors, and the old serial numbers were canceled. Used tractors in dealership hands and tractors owned by customers, received the extensive—and expensive—fixes. Total costs were enormous, but IH did its best to satisfy the customers.

IH Tractors Around the World

Truly, "International"

International Harvester began a program of establishing overseas tractor production in the late 1930s. Overseas manufacturing wasn't new to IH. The company had been operating in Norkopping, Sweden, since 1906, in Neuss, Germany, since 1909, and in other parts of the world since early in the century. But during the Great Depression, many nations had established protectionist policies that interfered heavily with the export business that IH had enjoyed. IH had to build new factories in these countries to maintain market share.

German Production

Two locations in Europe were selected for the start of tractor manufacture, Doncaster England, and Neuss, Germany. IH officials were not happy about producing

IH of Great Britain painted a few Super BMDs gold for their introduction at the Royal Agriculture Show. The direct-start diesels and increased horsepower proved popular, although row-crop tractors were not terribly popular in Britain. These tractors today are rare and desirable. State Historical Society of Wisconsin

77

The D-320 and D-324 were the midsize standard tractors in the German IH line at the end of the 1950s and were extremely popular. The "elephant" fenders were standard equipment in the German line. State Historical Society of Wisconsin

tractors in Nazi Germany, but the Nazi authorities had been making doing business in Germany with out manufacturing tractors there very difficult. It was a case of doing it or losing their entire investment. Neuss started production of F-12-G and I-12-Gs in 1937, although the industrial tractor lasted less than a year. It is not known how long tractor production lasted into the war, or if it continued after the German government seized the plant.

Neuss Works was nearly wiped off the face of the earth by Allied bombers and ground combat. The factory was considered 80 percent destroyed. Situated on an island in the Rhine River, the plant was easily recognizable from the air and on radar, resulting in more than 300 bomb hits. By Fowler McCormick's 1950 visit, the German IH workers had performed miracles. The stones were pulled out of the rubble one by one and rebuilt into an operating factory. The basements uncovered by the rubble removal were flooded. The machine tools that had fallen into the basements when buildings collapsed were removed from the water, cleaned and repaired,

and reassembled into an operation that shipped 450 F-12 descendants (Models FS and FG) in 1949.

During 1949, the FS was discontinued, while the FG became the basis for a new model called the FG-E. It was intended for export and fitted with streamlined sheet metal and a new nonferrous steering wheel, and for the first time in German production, it was painted red with aluminum-coated rims to match the rest of IH production. The Standard FG was available with FGE features, but only at an extra cost. Frugal German farmers still got gray tractors with the old sheet metal, but later in 1949 the FGE features became standard for FGs. A 6-volt electric starting system was added in December 1949.

The first week of January 1950 saw the release of the second batch of 50 preproduction FG tractors with MWM-produced, two-cylinder diesel engines. The second batch received improved engines and had streamlined fuel tanks, crown fenders, and a foot accelerator with a lock for belt pulley operation (no hand throttle). The model designation was changed to FGD-2.

The D-440, D-436, and D-430 lined up in April 1960. The D-440 was the first IH tractor to be equipped with a turbocharger, but it didn't remain in production long or in large numbers. State Historical Society of Wisconsin

Neuss Works released another batch of preproduction tractors in May 1950, this time with Neuss Works–produced, FG-D4, four-cylinder diesel engines. The new engines had an 80-millimeter bore and 4-inch stroke, with four-cycle combustion and 1,650 rpm yielding 23 horsepower at the flywheel. A precombustion chamber, fuel-injection system (with Bosch pump, of course) was used. The engine was direct starting, as opposed to the start-on gas system of American models. The cylinders were wet sleeve, and intake and exhaust manifolds were on opposite sides of the engine. The exhaust was designed to produce straight line scavenging. Ten preproduction engines were built, with four going into tractors. The rest were used in the labs for endurance and purchased parts testing, with one engine being used for spare parts.

As the FG-D4 moved toward production, the transmission gearing in all FG tractors was improved to handle the increased horsepower of the diesel engine. Another change came about in September 1950, with the decision to identify all non-U.S. products with a letter to identify the

country of manufacture. Neuss Works products were identified with a "D" for "Deutschland." The old FG-D4 became the DF ("F" for Farmall). The FG and FG-E were discontinued in favor of the 124-ci (2,045-cubic centimeter) diesel engine. Two basic models of DFs were produced: the DF-A with 9.00x40 tires and the DF-T with 11.25x24 tires. The tractors had slightly different transmissions and front axles. The DF entered regular production in November 1950 with other chassis improvements over the FG. The FG and FG-E were discontinued when the DF entered production. The DFs quickly built up an export trade worldwide.

The DF engines were available for field replacement of the old FG and FG-E carbureted engines as long as they were originally fitted with electric start. The DF chassis was modified in early 1951 to provide a front PTO. The DF diesel engine also was provided, with special parts, for the French-produced FC ("French C").

A smaller tractor first saw preproduction versions in July 1952. The DE had a three-cylinder diesel

The D-214, the D-217 Standard, and the D-217 Farmall are tractors from Neuss Works. These were the small tractors from the German line and were exported to many parts of Europe, Asia, and Africa. State Historical Society of Wisconsin

engine yielding 19.7 peak horsepower and 17.8 horsepower as set by the factory. A five-speed transmission was fitted with 8-32 rear tires. Special features included a differential lock, spring-mounted front axle, fender seats, front and rear trailer draw clevises, a three-point linkage, and a hydraulic lift. The first preproduction lot of 100 tractors was approved in September 1952. The name was modified slightly to DED, and the list of attachments was increased with front-wheel splash fenders, a weather cab for the operator, elephant ear fenders, and Category I and II three-point hitches in November. The attachment list for the DF was also improved with a weather cab at about the same time.

The DED story got a little more confused in December 1952. Another lot of 400 tractors was released. Although the decision said they were released for regular production, the text of the decision used the term preproduction for these tractors. In March 1953, 500 more tractors built to the preproduction standards were authorized. A new transmission case was designed for the DED production tractors, to be used after the preproduction tractors left production, that included a provision for independent PTO. A lot of 500 more preproduction tractors was authorized in late May 1953, and another 1,000 were authorized in early July. The tractor was renamed DED-3 and released for final production in December 1953. The year 1953 also saw a high-clearance DF, with special steering knuckles and improved-clearance front axle released in February.

The DGD was released for regular production in March 1953, with a 3 1/4x4 four-cylinder diesel operating at 1,750 rpm giving 27.6 horsepower. Double disk brakes were fitted, as was a five-speed transmission. The starting system used 12-volt Bosch components. A ZF steering mechanism was used. The special attachments were very similar to the DED, except that only a Category II three-point hitch was available. Although released for regular production, the first 475 were released as preproduction, followed by 300 more preproduction tractors in August.

The tractor was renamed DGD-4 and was finally released for regular production in December 1953.

After release, major variants and options flowed quickly. Weather Cabs were made available for both the DED-3 and DGD-4 in May 1954. A high-clearance version of the DED-3 and DGD-4 was released in February 1954. Rear tire equipment using 8-36 rear tires was intended for cultivation, while 11-28 tires were used in transport use on the DED-3 and transport and heavy tillage for the DGD-4. A 9-26 rear tire was also available for the DGD-4 for heavy tillage. All high-clearance attachments had a high-clearance front axle and a variety of front tires and were available either at the factory or as field attachments.

Five rice field DGD-4s were released as preproduction tractors in July 1954, with another five tractors being built in December. The rice field versions had a high-crop transmission (gearing adjusted to match larger tires), a reinforced high tire front axle, 13-30 rear tires, 6.00-20 front tires, and special parts to match larger rims to hubs. The tractors were produced for Pedro Martinto, S.A., in Lima, Peru.

The DED-3 and DGD-4 got some attachments of an American origin in late 1954. Fast Hitch attachments were made for the tractors, which were already available with three-point hitches, exactly the opposite of American history.

A limited production run of orchard DED-3 and DGD-4 tractors was authorized in early 1955. The tractor featured transmissions giving slow speeds, a lowered steering wheel and shortened lever, and sheet metal and steering wheel cowls produced by the Rag. E. Michelini firm of Ferrara, Italy, who ordered the tractors. Michelini was the Italian IH distributor.

The preproduction D-Cub-D was released in late June 1953. The engine was a two-cylinder, direct-starting diesel with 3 1/4x4 cylinders, known as the

This photograph is apparently of the Neuss Works experimental assembly area. There's an interesting looking hood in the foreground that never made it into production. State Historical Society of Wisconsin

DD-66. Horsepower was 14, running through a ZF five-speed transmission. ZF also supplied the steering gear. One hundred tractors were authorized at first, with another order of 900 following in early 1954.

The D-Cub-D was available with special attachments, including a spring-mounted front axle, fender seat, front-wheel splash seats, belt pulley, front and rear trailer hitches, hydraulic lifts, weather cab, elephant ear fenders, Category I three-point hitch, 12-volt starting system (6-volt was standard), steel wheels, and a swinging drawbar. On preproduction tractors, the final drives, rear-axle carriers, brakes, and pedals were supplied by ZF, but for production tractors (renamed DLD-2) the manufacture was taken over by IH to reduce costs. The DLD-2 was released

The 1954 Royal Agriculture Show also had red Super BMDs on display. Although many chassis parts were the same as the American Super M, the engine, injection pump, front axle, and many other parts were strictly British. State Historical Society of Wisconsin

for production September 25, 1954. A hydraulic lift was made available at the same time, with three-point hitches following shortly thereafter. The DLD-2, DED-3, and DGD-4 engines used a high degree of interchangeable parts, including sleeves, pistons, connecting rods, valvetrain, and main and rod bearings.

Changes to the German line began to occur in mid-1955. The DED-3 and DGD-4 received a six-speed transmission as regular equipment, while eight tractors with experimental eight-speed "Agriomatic" transmissions were released for testing. Super DED-3s and Super DGD-4s were released for production with larger engines and the six speeds, and then canceled before production actually began. The DF trac-

tor, the granddaddy of the German IH diesels, was discontinued in October 1955. In September 1956, the older DLD-2, DED-3, and DGD-4 were discontinued. All was in preparation for new, advanced tractors to be known as the D-Line.

A decision that received approval on December 19, 1955, authorized three tractors in the D-Line: the D-320, the 324, and the D-430. The 320 and 324 were essentially the same tractor with differences. The 320 had a 3 1/4x4 three-cylinder diesel producing 20 horsepower at 1,750 rpm. The engine was designated the DD-99, reflecting the displacement. The 324 had a 3 7/16x4 diesel, developing 24 horsepower at 1,900 rpm and designated the DD-111. Both tractors had a

B-275s were intended for agricultural markets in the Southeast, but many of them found their way into industrial uses as well. IH eventually made quite a business of shipping skidded British tractors into Louisville Works and adding parts for the industrial and ag markets. State Historical Society of Wisconsin

six-speed transmission, with first being a creeper gear. The 324 had a slightly larger fuel tank than the 320.

The D-430 had the same tank as the 324 but was a larger tractor. Styling was the same as the smaller tractors, but the D-430 had a 3 1/4x4 four-cylinder diesel, known as the DD-132, that developed 30 horsepower at 1,750 rpm. This tractor also had a six-speed transmission as standard, but the right-speed Agriomatic would be added as an option in March 1956 and for the D-320 and D-324 in August 1956. All three tractors could have a Fast Hitch attachment as well as three-point equipment and straight drawbars. A restyled radiator grille was authorized in February 1956. Rice field

D-430s were authorized for full production (export only, of course) in November 1956, while special stripped-down D-430s for the Philippines were authorized in May 1957.

Two new small tractors joined the line in mid-1956. The D-212 and D-217 were row-crop and utility versions carrying on in the two-cylinder diesel Cub and DLD-2 tradition. The D-212 was the smaller version of the pair, with a 3 1/4x4 two-cylinder, direct-start, DD-66 diesel engine delivering 12 horsepower at 1,750 rpm. The D-217 had a 3 7/16x4 two-cylinder diesel, designated the DD-74, that delivered 17 horsepower at 1,900 rpm. Both tractors had six-speed transmissions with a first speed creeper gear.

The Farmall B-450 diesel was descended from the BMD and was the large row-crop tractor in the British line. Since the British didn't need a whole lot of row-crop tractors, a large export market was built up, including a few brought quietly into the United States. State Historical Society of Wisconsin

The D-217 had larger tires than the D-212 and delivered slightly higher speeds. The D-212 had slightly higher ground clearance (435 millimeters) than the D-217 (380 millimeters) while delivering a smaller turning radius, despite greater overall length (4 centimeters, but the wheelbase was identical). The D-217 tank held more than 2 gallons more fuel than the D-212.

The first modern, production IH tractor to be supercharged was released in August 1957. The McCormick International D-440 was released only for limited production. Although experiments with supercharging had taken place since about 1908 with some regularity, the D-440 with Roots blower was the first to hit the customer. Two hundred tractors were

released in the preliminary run. The 3 1/4x4 four-cylinder diesel (similar to that of the D-430) produced 40 horsepower at the flywheel (1,900 rpm), versus 30 horsepower for the D-430. Final production release for the D-440 was granted in April 1958.

Utility versions of the two-cylinder tractors were introduced in early 1958. The D-214 and "redesigned" D-217 had similar mechanicals to the Farmall versions, which were redesignated "D-212-F" and "D-217-F." The D-214 actually had 14 horsepower to the D-212's 12, mainly from raising the rpm slightly, but the increase was soon made for the D-212 as well. Another intriguing and mysterious version of the D-212 was released in early 1957. The "Dairy Special" had revised hood sheets, different number panels, and different tire sizes than the D-212. Both the Dairy Special and the D-212-F were discontinued in October 1959, with the decision noting that the D-212-F had not been produced in the previous year.

A limited run of another new tractor was authorized in late 1958. One hundred D-436s were authorized, 10 of which were part of a production run of the D-430/440 family. The new tractors featured a DD-148, 3 7/16x4 four-cylinder engine, delivering 36 horsepower at 1,900 rpm. The tractor had the Agriomatic eight-speed transmission and was similar in appearance and dimensions to the earlier 430/440s. The 436 was approved for full production in May 1959. In late 1959, a special high-clearance D-430-S and D-436-S was approved for the Philippines. The new attachment increased crop clearance by 5 inches. These tractors were basically kits, with assembly (including the addition of a lot of Philippine parts) in the Philippines.

By 1960, IH Germany had risen from the 27th largest farm equipment manufacturer in Germany to the 2nd largest.

English Production

IH purchased a large site well suited for tractor and implement manufacture in Doncaster, England, in 1938. Construction of the factory was nearly complete when Great Britain entered World War II in 1939. The factory was taken over for wartime production by the British government until 1945. IH's delegation surveying the European situation and the old IH properties after the war recommended purchasing the factory back from the government. The decision was again made to produce tractors in Britain, but progress toward the goal was slow at first. Tom Williams, minister of agriculture, issued a challenge to Doncaster Works in March 1948. If IH

IH of Great Britain's line filled out nicely in the late 1950s. The B-275 provided power for Britain's many small farms and a large export market, while the B-450 provided sturdy power for large farms in a Farmall and a Standard version. State Historical Society of Wisconsin

could get tractors into production in 18 months he would personally drive the first tractor off the line. IH beat him by a month. Williams appeared to drive the tractor off the line in very proper British morning attire.

Tractor production in Doncaster began in 1949 with the BM, although it was still decaled and known as the M until late 1951. The British product differed in many ways from the American product to match the local market. The wide front axle had the tie rods in the rear and a revised mounting. While the tractor originally did have a high U.S.-made parts content,

Tractors on the assembly line in St. Dizier, France, in 1960. St. Dizier still makes (at this writing) transmissions and other components for Case-IH European operations. State Historical Society of Wisconsin

both design and content became increasingly British as time went by. The first "100 percent British" M was made in 1952. Three-point hitches were made available in the early 1950s.

All early BMs were carbureted engines using engines similar to American production, but the market soon demanded a diesel. Experiments focused on "conversion" engines that would use many of the same parts in carbureted and diesel engines to reduce parts counts and the need for expensive tooling. At first, the conversion experiments concentrated on the original 3 7/8x5 1/4 engine, but in early 1952, efforts turned to a 4x5 1/4 engine. Diesel and distillate versions were experimented with, and in December 1952, a direct-start

diesel with glow plug–assisted start was first produced in the new size, known as the BD-264. A distillate (known as TVO for tractor vaporizing oil) version, known as the BC-264, was also introduced. The new engines were introduced in early 1953, without a change in model designation at the time for the Model BM (the "Model" was added earlier to avoid interference with a Swedish brand name) while the diesel was introduced as the Farmall BMD.

The large bore engine gave an opportunity to increase horsepower, but much work needed to be done. Doncaster engineers raced to prepare a new tractor for the Royal Agricultural Society of England Show in July 1953. Queen Elizabeth II had just been crowned in June, and England was buzzing with

An FU-265 diesel utility tractor pulling a dynamometer tractor at St. Dizier. The dyno tractor looks to have been built from one of the French C variants. The engine cylinders would have been used to generate load, which would have been measured by electronics in the hitch. State Historical Society of Wisconsin

excitement as any festivity that year went all out to help celebrate. IH's British engineers redesigned the tractor to handle 50 horsepower, including a new clutch, transmission, and main frame. Production began just before the show, with deliveries beginning just after. Several of the new Farmall Super BMDs were painted gold to celebrate the coronation. Shortly after the show's end, IH Doncaster Works held a ceremony of its own, to celebrate the 10,000th Farmall tractor since September 1949 and the 1,000th diesel

tractor. Carbureted Super BMs were introduced at the same time.

The next year at the Royal Show, another new IH tractor was introduced. The SBWD-6 and SBW-6 were the British versions of the American Super WD-6 and SW-6 channel frame tractors. Using a high number of Super BM and BMD parts, the tractors were introduced for higher horsepower applications that did not need or did not want row-crop features.

The Farmall F-265-D was a popular French tractor when this photo was taken in March 1960. What looks like a fender seat is located on the left side of the tractor. Tractors were, and still are, used as road transportation in Europe and accommodations were made for riders, such as they were. State Historical Society of Wisconsin

The B-250 entered production in 1956. Known as "The Little Giant," the tractor was produced at IH's new Bradford Works, which was purchased from the Jowett Company, manufacturer of cars and light trucks. Many of the Jowett workers were subsequently employed by IH. Soon after introduction, Bradford was turning out 50 B-250s a day, with a year's backlog of orders on the books. The diesel tractors featured a 3 3/8x4 engine designated the BD-144. A five-speed transmission was standard, but an eight-speed transmission with IPTO was also available. An industrial version followed in early 1958. Early in 1959, changes were made in the B-250 to use as many B-275 parts as possible to reduce cost. Preproduction B-250 and

B-275 tractors with draft control and depth stops were released in August 1958.

Two new families of tractors became available in 1958. The B-275 entered production at Bradford Works. A bigger brother to the B-250, preproduction B-275s featured a slightly larger BD-152 3 3/8x4 1/4 diesel engine. For production tractors, a BD-144-A engine set for 32 horsepower was fitted. Engine changes included a variety of changes to valves, cam profiles, ventilation, and an integral hydraulic pump. The eight-speed transmission was again used. Export tractors could be fitted with an increased capacity radiator. In mid-1958, high-clearance versions of the B-250 and B-275 were released for Australia, and different high-crop B-275s were released for other

The FV-165-D was the small French diesel vineyard tractor. The tractors were very narrow and small to fit between rows of grapevines and other similar crops, rather than under trees like American orchard and grove types. State Historical Society of Wisconsin

markets. The tractors had higher front axles, larger rear wheels and tires, and different three-point hitches.

The new large tractor was the B-450. The B-450 standard was an updated version of the BSWD-6, with a integral live hydraulic lift, a differential lock, disc brakes, and an updated BD-264 engine putting out 55 horsepower. A row-crop version followed in 1959, using a Super BMD front end and a B450 back end. The name of the tractor changed several times, as the term Farmall was applied and then removed. Much like their American counterparts of the era, the British large tractors ran into extensive transmission problems in the late 1950s. American-designed gearing was replaced by British gearing, which differed mainly in material used. Distillate versions were made available in 1959.

In the late 1950s, the high cost of American manufacture compared to low-cost British labor, combined with small British diesels that had no American counterpart, saw British tractors going across the Atlantic to the North American market, following a path blazed by both Fordson and Ferguson.

The British invasion of North America began in 1957. IH of Canada started importing the B-250 to meet the demand for a small diesel tractor. It quickly became the most popular British tractor sold in Canada. By 1959, the B-250 had been replaced by

The McCormick International Farmall F-135-D was a small diesel row-crop tractor that would have been roughly equivalent to the 140 in the United States. State Historical Society of Wisconsin

the B-275, which met the same unusually fine acceptance from Canadian farmers. April 1959 saw the start of shipments from IH's Bradford, England, plant to Jacksonville, Florida. The main market in the United States for the British tractors was in the Southeast, where small, economical diesel tractors were perfect for the small farms found there. The sales price in the United States was $2,802 at the port. It was equipped with the IH 144-ci diesel engine putting out 35 horsepower, eight forward and two reverse gears, constant-running PTO, live hydraulics, three-point hitch, disc brakes, 12-volt electrics, and a differential lock.

Some other uniquely British programs were undertaken in the late 1950s. The most interesting was the provision of conversion kits for older M and BM tractors to convert them into direct-start Super BMDs. Kits to convert American Ms to Super BMD were produced and shipped to Mexico.

French Production

International Harvester started producing farm equipment in France in 1909 at Croix, where grain and harvesting machinery was produced. McCormick had sold in France for decades before, and both McCormick and Deering had displayed Automowers at the Paris World's Fair in 1900, so France was familiar territory. Another IH factory was built at Montataire in the 1930s to build plows, tillage equipment, and planting equipment.

The Super Cub was the successor to the French Cub, but maintained a resemblance to the American 1954–1956 Cubs, even in the March 1960 photograph at the St. Dizier engineering department. State Historical Society of Wisconsin

These plants were taken over by the Germans during World War II for production of agricultural and military implements, and accordingly, the plants received their share of attention from Allied bombers and ground forces. Croix escaped fairly unscathed, but Montataire was heavily damaged. After the war, IH took control back and began to rebuild and modernize the plants. Tractor production started to receive attention, and IH of France (known as CIMA) selected an abandoned factory in St. Dizier, located in a region known for its foundries and metal fabricating (the Statue of Liberty was produced less than 5 miles from the plant). Marshall Plan money made the expansion feasible in the recovering econo-

my. CIMA paid the government French francs, which the government used in repair, highway construction, and so on. The government, in turn, used the Marshall Plan American dollars to purchase the machinery CIMA needed from overseas (of course, mainly from America), reducing postwar inflation.

St. Dizier got into production in 1951 with the FC (not to be confused with the American C, which used a serial prefix of "FC" on the serial number plate). The FC was quite similar to its American cousin, but did not yet have Touch Control. It did have the C-113 engine, produced in the United States. In 1952, an optional DF-124 diesel engine made at IH's Neuss Works was added, resulting in a tractor known as the FCN. The diesel was based on the C-113 and produced 24 horsepower. The engine was a direct start, like all the German diesels.

1952 also saw the introduction of the Super FC. The carbureted versions of this tractor had the C-123 engine, still produced in the United States. Touch Control hydraulics were finally added as well. This tractor didn't last long in production, being replaced by the Super FCC in 1953. The Super FCC featured a French-designed and produced engine, the FC-123, which developed 30 horsepower at 2,000 rpm. The Diesel FCN was also replaced in 1953 by the FCD. The new tractor used a French-produced FD-123

diesel engine that was based on the French-designed gas FC-123. It developed 28 horsepower at 1,800 rpm. The Super FCD added the Touch Control hydraulics in the diesel line as well. Unlike the American Touch Control, the French tractors had a system by which the Touch Control was fitted with linkages for three-point hitches.

Utility versions of the Super FCC and the Super FCD entered production in 1954. The compact tractors used the same engines as their Farmall ancestors but with rearranged chassis. Both the diesel and carbureted Utility tractors were sold in Vineyard versions as well. The vineyard tractors (known as the Vineyard

Super Cubs on the paint line. Compared to the American paint lines in the 1940s, which already had water walls, the French line looks a little more primitive but was faced with a much lower workload than Louisville Works, which was planned for 400 tractors a day. State Historical Society of Wisconsin

The AM-7 was based on the AM, but featured the American two-tone styling, three-point hitches, and other advantages, including direct start in the decals. IH's Australian operations were small and didn't update the basic design for several decades. State Historical Society of Wisconsin

Super FCC and the Vineyard Super FCD) were very narrow tractors (42 inches, as opposed to 68 inches for the Utility) with few protrusions, but did not have wheel-enclosing fenders or shields like American orchard tractors. In fact, the Vineyard tractors had more in common with shop mules produced in the United States.

A new hydraulic system was introduced for the FC descendants in 1958. The "Modulor" hydraulic system featured draft sensing for the first time. The tractor model numbers were changed to the F-235 to reflect the new system. These tractors, including the Farmall F-235, the Farmall F-235D, the Utility FU-235, the FU-235D, the Vineyard FV-235, and the FV-235D, also featured eight forward speeds (six field, two road), two reverse gears, and live PTO.

In 1959, the F-235 family received a restyling and extensive changes in the chassis. The newly renamed F-265 family was available in all three French variants (Farmall, Utility, Orchard) and featured torque amplification and a differential lock. A new, larger engine, the FD-136, was introduced.

A new size of tractors entered into production at St. Dizier in 1955. Farmall Cubs were built with the FC-60 engine (with a distributor) and styling similar to the 1954–1956 Cubs produced in the United States. The French Cub was replaced in 1958 by a Super Farmall Cub, which had minor changes.

Another new size of tractor entered production in early 1957. The F-135D was produced with a DD-74 two-cylinder diesel engine (manufactured at Neuss Works) producing 17 horsepower. The tractor filled the gap between the Cub and the F-235s. A ZF six-speed transmission was used with the tractor, which was very similar to the German Farmall D-217, sharing some chassis and hydraulics parts. The F-135D eventually became the F-137D.

For a few years, starting in 1957, St. Dizier produced a large tractor, the F-335. The tractor had a four-cylinder diesel engine and was similar in size to the American 330s and 350s, although the engine was direct start.

Australian Production

IH's involvement down under went back to the days of Cyrus McCormick and reaper trade in the 1850s. IH built a factory for production of agricultural implements, with room to expand into tractor and truck manufacture, in 1938 in Australia. Tractor production at Geelong Works began in 1948 with the W-6, and the Ms came in 1949. Expansion of the IH facilities was made possible by a plan where IH sold 97 TD-18A and TD-24 crawlers to the Australian government in 1950. Instead of getting paid in American dollars, the government paid IH in Australian pounds, which were then used in IH construction projects, including expansion in tractors and farm equipment and an entirely new truck plant. The AW-6 and Farmall AM entered production in 1949, and the AOS-6 entered production in 1953. The SAM, SAM-D, SAW-6, SAWD-6, and AOS-6 followed in 1954. The AW-7D and AW-7K entered production in 1957, and the AM-7K and AM-7D joined them in 1958 (although limited production of the SAM and the SAM-D occurred in 1959 and 1960). The AIS-6, was produced in 1959 and 1960, the AI-7 and AI-7D were produced in 1959 only, and the SAI-6 and SAID-6 were produced in 1958 and 1959.

Philippine Production

IH entered the Philippine market in 1904, with the purchase of a Scots firm, Macleod and Company, to supply hemp to its twine mills. After World War II, the new nation of the Philippines suffered from the

The AW-7 was the Australian standard tractor of its day, obviously based on the American W series. Australia had expanses of semi-arid land similar to the Great Plains wheat areas of the United States. They invented much of modern combine technology, and IH manufactured combines based on Australian designs for both the U.S. and Australian markets in the 1910s. State Historical Society of Wisconsin

same American dollar shortages as much of the rest of the world did, so a "Filipinization" program was initiated to bring in jobs and keep scarce dollars. In early 1957, a pilot lot of 31 D-430s were built using imported components from Neuss and local labor and certain locally produced components. In November 1957, IH began importing D-430s as knocked-down kits, with certain parts deducted. IH purchased locally made parts such as tires and manufactured some parts locally such as sheet metal, front weights, mufflers, and other assorted components. Soon 54 percent of the tractor by price was made locally. D-436s also received the same treatment. The tractors had Fast Hitch and high-clearance front axles. A cage-type wetlands dual steel wheel was used outboard of the pneumatic rear tires.

Index